HELPERS IN OUR COMMUNITY

BUS DRIVERS

CHRISTINE HONDERS

New York

Published in 2020 by The Rosen Publishing Group, Inc.
29 East 21st Street, New York, NY 10010

First Edition

Editor: Greg Roza
Book Design: Reann Nye

Photo Credits: Cover, p.1 New Africa/Shutterstock.com; pp. 4–22 Abstractor/Shutterstock.com; p. 5 Africa Studio/Shutterstock.com; p. 7 Photo By Tom Carter/Photographer's Choice/Getty Images Plus/Getty Images; p. 9 Pat Shrader/Shutterstock.com; p. 11 Andersen Ross Photography Inc/DigitalVision/Getty Images; p. 13 Image Source/Getty Images; p. 15 Copyright Artem Vorobiev/Moment Open/Getty Images; p.17 Monkey Business Images/Shutterstock.com; p. 19 Jaren Jai Wicklund/Shutterstock.com; p. 21 K.Sorokin/Shutterstock.com; p. 21kali9/E+/Getty Images.

Library of Congress Cataloging-in-Publication Data

Names: Honders, Christine, author.
Title: Bus drivers / Christine Honders.
Description: New York : PowerKids Press, [2020] | Series: Helpers in our community | Includes index.
Identifiers: LCCN 2019011611| ISBN 9781725308107 (pbk.) | ISBN 9781725308121 (library bound) | ISBN 9781725308114 (6 pack)
Subjects: LCSH: Bus drivers–Juvenile literature.
Classification: LCC HD8039.M8 H66 2020 | DDC 388.3/22023–dc23
LC record available at https://lccn.loc.gov/2019011611

Manufactured in the United States of America

CPSIA Compliance Information: Batch #CWPK20. For Further Information contact Rosen Publishing, New York, New York at 1-800-237-9932.

CONTENTS

Who Gets You There?

On most days, many kids go to school and many adults go to work. On days off, many people like going out with friends and family. Who can take you places every day of the week? The bus driver takes you where you need to go.

Making Streets Safer

People who take city buses are in fewer **accidents** on the road. Studies show that taking **public transportation** is much safer than riding in a car. Taking the bus is one of the safest ways to get to school.

18 LANGLEY PARK
025607
RIDE ON
025607
RIDE ON
NEW FLIGHTS TO PANAMA CITY BEACH, FLORIDA

Good Drivers

Buses are safer than cars, in part, because they move more slowly. Sometimes, they have special lanes that cars can't use. School buses have high, padded seats that are close together. This may keep riders safer in a crash. Bus drivers also must have special training for their job.

EMERGENCY DOOR

Bus Driver Training

Drivers must train to learn how to drive big **vehicles** such as buses. They learn the rules. They learn to figure out what's wrong if a bus breaks down. They also learn what to do to keep everyone safe if there's a problem.

School Bus Rules

School buses have special rules. School bus drivers make sure students follow the rules! Stay in your seat until the bus gets to your stop. Talk quietly and don't yell. It's your job to follow the rules to keep yourself safe on the bus.

Busing in the Big City

City bus drivers know how many people can safely ride the bus at once. They learn their **routes** and when to reach each stop. They know how to drive with lots of other vehicles. They watch for people walking or riding bikes in the street.

NOT IN SERVICE

A Friendly Face

The bus driver may be one of the first people you see in the morning. Does it make your day better if they're smiling? Some bus drivers get to know their riders well. They have good people skills. They're friendly with their riders and make them feel **comfortable**.

Helping People

Some people need buses because they don't have cars. Buses may have special tools so people with **disabilities** can ride on them. Buses also help keep unsafe drivers off the road. If someone is too tired to drive, they can take a bus.

Helping Our Planet

Bus drivers help our planet! More people on the bus means fewer cars on the road. That means less **pollution** in the air. Taking the bus also cuts down on how much gas we use. Also, more cities now use electric buses.

ECO BUS
1

Keeping the Community Moving

If you ride a bus, you expect the bus to be there every day to pick you up and take you home. Buses safely take people to school, to work, and to places all over the country. But that couldn't happen without the driver. Bus drivers keep our community moving!

GLOSSARY

accident: A sudden event that's not planned or wanted.

comfortable: At ease.

disability: A condition that limits a person's abilities.

pollution: Something that makes land, water, or air dirty and unsafe to use.

public transportation: Something used by the people in the community as a way of getting from one place to another.

route: A road or course of travel from one place to another.

vehicle: A machine used to carry people or goods from one place to another.

INDEX

WEBSITES

Due to the changing nature of Internet links, PowerKids Press has developed an online list of websites related to the subject of this book. This site is updated regularly. Please use this link to access the list: www.powerkidslinks.com/hioc/drivers